Mary, Woman of Prayer

To Noreen.
From Gerry.

"Good Health & God Bless"

FR MICHAEL CAMPBELL OSA

Mary, Woman of Prayer

Meditations on the Mysteries of the Rosary

ST PAULS

Photographs by: Durand, 6 Avenue Mgr Schoepfer, Lourdes

Published by ST PAULS (by Westminster Cathedral) London SW1P 1EP

Copyright © Fr Michael Campbell OSA, 2007

ISBN 978-0-85439-736-5

Set by Tukan DTP, Stubbington, Fareham, UK
Printed by AGAM, Cuneo, Italy

Our Lady of Lourdes

Foreword

When I think of the great Mysteries of the Faith, the image of a diamond comes to my mind. Hold a diamond at different angles to the same source of light and different colours emerge at each turn; piercing white; a burning red; the freshness of green; and the warmth of yellow. Each one is a complete expression of the juxtaposition of light and colour, yet none of them exhausts the potential for beauty which lies within.

No matter how hard we try, no words or art or music can fully convey the inner truths of our faith. The ancient creeds and books of theology, our prayers and our hymns attempt, in different ways, to capture the wonder and awe of the revelation of God in the person of Jesus Christ. Each one helps us to explore the Mystery of Faith. Important as it is to try to understand these teachings, the ultimate truth is that each of us is held in a relationship of love with God our Father, through our communion with his son, by the power of the Holy Spirit.

One of the great devotional treasures of the Church is the Rosary. One tradition is that the form of the Rosary was revealed to St Dominic in the early thirteenth century. The fifteen mysteries have truly been described as an extended meditation on the Scriptures, seen through the eyes of Mary. From the Annunciation of the Incarnation to the Coronation of Our Lady in Heaven, we make our own the salvation won for us through the Passion, Death and Resurrection of our Lord.

The new Mysteries of Light composed by Pope John Paul II take us to the heart of the Scriptures and of the sacramental life of the Church. "Do whatever he tells you," is a powerful message to all who seek to follow the example of Mary, the Woman of Faith. Mary is indeed, "...the highest honour of our race," in her conformity to the will of God.

In this beautiful book of Meditations, *Mary, Woman of Prayer,* Fr Michael Campbell OSA has given us new and enriching reflections on the journey of faith which we each have to make. Where better to use them than during a pilgrimage to Lourdes? That holy place has been hallowed by the prayers of faithful people over the last one hundred and fifty years. As we join together in prayer on pilgrimage, the words of the preface for the Assumption of Our Lady into heaven shine light on the faith and the hope we all share. She was "…taken up to heaven to be the beginning and the pattern of the church in its perfection, and a sign of hope and comfort for your people on their pilgrim way."

† Bishop George Stack
Auxiliary Bishop
Westminster Archdiocese

How to pray the Rosary

The Rosary is made up of decades. A decade is one Our Father, followed by ten Hail Marys and a Glory Be. It is usual to say five decades at a time.

Begin with the Sign of the Cross. Pray the Apostles' Creed holding the crucifix and continue on the straight piece of the Rosary with one Our Father, three Hail Marys and a Glory Be.

To start the first decade, pray one Our Father, ten Hail Marys and finish the first decade by saying the Glory be and the Fatima Prayer. By saying five decades of the Rosary, you will complete one complete circuit of the beads. To finish, when you have completed your chosen number of decades, pray the Hail Holy Queen.

As you say each decade, using the Meditations in this booklet will help you to concentrate on the various events of the life of Our Lord and his Blessed Mother.

The Joyful Mysteries

*'Inspired by your example and with the help of your prayers,
may we listen attentively to God's word …'*

The Annunciation

The angel said to her, 'Do not be afraid Mary, for you have found favour with God. Behold you will conceive in your womb and bear a son, and you shall call his name Jesus.' Luke 1:30-31

The Angel Gabriel came to Mary as a messenger from heaven. God's chosen moment had now come to send his Son into the world. Being the object of God's special favour, 'full of grace', Mary need have no fear. The Son to whom she would give birth would be the long promised One from the royal line of King David, and his reign would endure forever. The unique and wonderful manner of the child's conception, the angel tells Mary, will be the work of God's Holy Spirit. In great generosity of faith Mary accepts the words of the angel as God's will, and modestly acknowledges that she is the humble handmaid of the Lord. In her readiness to obey God's will, the Virgin Mary can serve as the model for all of us believers. She is also the image of what the Church is called to be: both a hearer and a doer of God's word.

PRAYER

Mary, virgin of Nazareth, at the Annunciation you opened your heart to God's call, accepting the angel's message with faith and with deep submission to the divine will. Inspired by your example and with the help of your prayers, may we listen attentively to God's word which is ever alive and new, so that it may be a lamp for our steps and a light for our path in our everyday life.

*'...Intercede for us, your children, that we may see your Son
in the faces of those around us, especially the sick and suffering.'*

The Visitation

'When Elizabeth heard Mary's greeting, the child in her womb leapt for joy, and Elizabeth was filled with the Holy Spirit.' Luke 1:41

On learning of Elizabeth's pregnancy, Mary sets out for the hill country of Judah to be close to her cousin in time of need. As Mary enters the house John the Baptist leaps for joy in his mother's womb. The infant John is aware of being in the presence of the Messiah, now present in the womb of Mary, and knows that God's salvation is near at hand. Already, John is fulfilling his ministry of showing Christ to the world. Speaking in the power of God's Holy Spirit, Elizabeth proclaims that Mary is singularly blessed among women, and that God's favour will rest upon the child she is carrying, 'the fruit of her womb'. Elizabeth warmly commends Mary for her faith, for her firm belief that the promises made by God through the angel Gabriel would come to pass. We look to Mary, woman of faith and friend to Elizabeth, as we strive to love God and our neighbour as ourselves.

PRAYER

Mary our Mother, you hastened to be with Elizabeth in her hour of need. Through your faith, active in good works, God's saving purpose for the human race was coming to pass in the child whom you had conceived. Intercede for us, your children, that we may see your Son in the faces of those around us, especially the sick and suffering. With the help of your prayers, let us too hasten to our neighbour in time of need.

The Basilica – Lourdes

The Birth of Our Lord

And she gave birth to a son, her first-born. And wrapping him in swaddling clothes she laid him in a manger, for there was no room for them at the inn. Luke 2:7

The Evangelist Luke describes in simple outline the scene of the first Christmas. The Creator of the world is laid in a humble manger, surrounded by the love of his mother and Joseph, rather than by material comforts. Told of his birth by the angels, shepherds were the first to acknowledge the birth of the One who would become our good shepherd. The shepherds related to Mary and Joseph the wonderful things they had just witnessed, and Mary is said to have kept and pondered them in her heart. As we marvel at the birth in time of the eternal Son of God, we remember that, like Mary, we also are called to a sense of wonder and contemplation, pondering prayerfully in our heart the awesome mystery of the Word become flesh and who made his home among us.

PRAYER

Father, touch our hearts and let us experience the infinite depths of your love when you graced us with the gift of your only-begotten Son. Enlighten our minds to understand that by his sharing in our humanity we have become your sons and daughters, privileged to call you Father. Like Mary, may we learn to treasure these wonderful truths of faith and know that at all times you are ever for us the Father of mercies and the God of all consolation.

Immaculate Conception

The Presentation of Our Lord in the Temple

As his father and mother wondered at the things that were being said about him, Simeon blessed them and said to his mother, 'Behold this child is set for the rise and fall of many in Israel, and will be a sign of contradiction. And a sword will pierce your own soul so that the secret thoughts of many hearts will be laid bare.' Luke 1:33-35

Faithful to the law of Moses, Mary and Joseph bring the infant Jesus to the temple to present him to the Lord. There they encounter the saintly Simeon who had waited his whole life for this moment. Inspired by the Holy Spirit the old man recognised the child as the Messiah, destined to be the light of the nations and the glory of God's people, Israel. Mary would be called to play her part in this mission of her Son, a role that would entail pain and suffering for her. Simeon prophesied that the child would encounter opposition and be rejected by many. His prophecy of a sword piercing his mother's heart, was a thinly veiled but powerful reference to Christ's sufferings and Mary's share in those sufferings, witnessed by her presence at the foot of the cross. We look to the Mother of the Saviour for the courage to face the troubles of life and to believe, as she did, that in God's loving design our sufferings will never be in vain.

PRAYER

Holy Spirit, Spirit of the Father and the Son, you inspired Simeon to come to the Temple and hold the Saviour of the world in his arms. He yearned to see the dawning of the messianic age before he would die, and you answered the prayer of your faithful servant. Holy Spirit, inspire us in our day, as Simeon once did, to point out Christ to the world, courageously to acknowledge him as the One sent from the Father to be Emmanuel, God-with-us. Overshadow us with your divine power, as you overshadowed Mary, that the Catholic faith may remain strong in us and that we may bear faithful witness to it.

Pope John Paul II blesses the sick

The Finding of the Child Jesus in the Temple

And after three days they found him in the Temple, seated among the teachers, listening to them and putting questions to them. Luke 1:46

It was during a visit to Jerusalem for the annual Passover feast that the child Jesus at the age of twelve became separated from his parents and was lost. The pain and distress of Mary his mother can hardly be imagined, and the prophetic words of Simeon that a sword would pierce her heart were beginning to come true. When asked why he had done this to them, the reply of the child Jesus left them puzzled: 'Did you not know that I must be busy with my Father's affairs?' Even as a boy Jesus was conscious of his divine identity as the Son of the Father. He was Mary's Son, but God's as well. The Evangelist tells us that his parents did not understand what Jesus said to them, but that deep in her heart Mary kept everything. The boy Jesus would mature and grow to manhood under the watchful eye of Mary, and through living close to Jesus she herself would grow in faith. Mary was called to a life of faith by remaining close to Jesus throughout her life. Her example remains the pattern and model for believers of every generation.

PRAYER

Holy Mother, Mary, you experienced pain when your son Jesus was lost, and your joy knew no limits when you found him again. Be the support and comfort of all mothers who are anxious for the welfare of their children. Give them wise counsel when they are in doubt, courage when they are afraid, and show them understanding when things go wrong. Be a mother to us all, keep us from danger, be with us now and especially at the hour of death.

The
Mysteries
of Light

'May your love, poured into our hearts through the Holy Spirit,
help us to lead lives worthy of the grandeur of our
Christian vocation.'

The Baptism of the Lord

At that time Jesus came from Nazareth in Galilee and was baptised by John in the Jordan. As he came up out of the water he saw the heavens opened and the Spirit descending on him like a dove. A voice was heard from heaven, 'You are my beloved Son, in you I am well pleased.'

Mark 1:9-11

Jesus comes to John to be baptised and so begin the work for which he has come into the world. In a wonderful act of humility the Son of God joins the crowds who flock to John to confess their sins and receive his baptism. The remarkable events which took place on the occasion of Christ's baptism are intended to deepen our understanding of who he really is. With the opening of the heavens the divine involvement in the life of Christ is underscored, while the descent of the Spirit suggests the gift of divine power for the mission he was about to undertake. The Father addresses Christ personally, affirming that he is his beloved Son, and much loved by the Father. The public ministry that Christ would now undertake is fully in accord with the Father's will. We recall our own baptism, through which we became sons and daughters of the Father, members of the body of Christ, and anointed by the Holy Spirit to bear witness to him in the world.

PRAYER

Lord Jesus Christ, your baptism in the river Jordan is the pattern of all Christian baptism, for when we are baptised we become the adopted sons and daughters of your Father and receive the spiritual anointing of the Holy Spirit. Through the waters of baptism, sanctified by your cross and resurrection, you call us to die to sin and selfishness and live the new life of the Spirit. Each day you invite us to make good our baptismal promises and so continue your saving presence in the world. May your love, poured into our hearts through the Holy Spirit, help us to lead lives worthy of the grandeur of our Christian vocation.

Pope John Paul II

The Marriage Feast of Cana

This was the first of Jesus' signs, which he performed at Cana in Galilee.
He revealed his glory, and his disciples believed in him. John 2:11

It was at the request of his mother Mary that Jesus worked his first miracle at a wedding feast in Cana. For him the hour of his public manifestation to Israel had not arrived yet he acceded to his mother's wishes, with the result that ordinary water was turned into the finest wine. For the evangelist John this miracle disclosed a deeper meaning, that of a sign through which Jesus revealed the glory that was uniquely his as the Son of God. One of the characteristics of the messianic age, according to the prophet Amos, would be an abundance of new wine [Amos 8:13]. The miracle at Cana was a sign that with the presence of Jesus Christ the messianic age had now dawned. John records how the faith of Jesus' disciples was strengthened by the sign they had just witnessed. We pray for that same insight of faith as we meditate on the many miracles the Lord Jesus worked. To obtain that grace for us, we invoke the intercession of Mary his mother, at whose request Jesus performed his first miracle.

PRAYER

Lord Jesus, through the wonder of your miracles you revealed your power, and caused your divine nature to shine through your human nature. At Cana, in the mystery of the water made wine, you gave a sign that the old order was passing and the new had come. Give us the vision to see your glory manifested again in our day. You are present to your Church in her ministry of word and sacrament, and are to be seen in the everyday faithfulness of so many of your people. Deepen our faith, Lord, in your abiding presence among us, until we see you face to face and drink the new wine of the kingdom of your Father together with all our brothers and sisters.

'Jesus, our Lord and Saviour, by your ministry of teaching and healing, you reached out to those who were afflicted and without hope.'

The Proclamation of the Gospel and the call to holiness

And he was given the scroll of the prophet Isaiah. He opened it and found the place where it was written, ' The Spirit of the Lord is upon me, wherefore he has anointed me. He has sent me to bring good news to the poor, to proclaim liberty to captives, to give sight to the blind, freedom to those who are oppressed, and to proclaim a year of favour from the Lord'. He said to them, 'Today this text is fulfilled as you listen.' Luke 4:17-19,21

The saving mission of Jesus is summed up in these words of the prophet Isaiah. Christ, the anointed One of the Lord, saw his own life's work expressed in these lofty prophetic statements. He would cheer the hearts of the poor and marginalised with a message of good news, assuring them of God's care and love for them. Central to Christ's preaching would be the closeness of God, and that religious and class differences counted for nothing in his sight. In fact, it was to those who felt themselves to be non-religious and distant from God that he gave renewed hope and inspiration, and he would even come to be known as the friend of sinners and tax-collectors. He could speak with authority because he was anointed with God's own Spirit, as were the kings, prophets and priests in the story of Israel. With the appearance of Christ a new and final age has now dawned for God's people. In the sacrament of Confirmation we too were anointed with the Spirit of the Lord and appointed to be ambassadors for Christ to the world.

PRAYER

Jesus, our Lord and Saviour, by your ministry of teaching and healing you reached out to those who were afflicted and without hope. You broke down barriers and offered the free gift of your Father's love to everyone without exception. You renewed spirits that were crushed and restored bodies that were broken. You sowed the seeds of God's kingdom and assured us that its progress could not be halted. You yourself were the grain of wheat that fell into the ground and died and so yielded a marvellous harvest. In union with you may our lives too bear a rich harvest that is both spiritual and material, advancing your kingdom which is a kingdom of truth and life, a kingdom of holiness and grace, and a kingdom of justice, love and peace.

'...sustain and nurture our faith with the vision of your heavenly glory...'

The Transfiguration

As he prayed, the aspect of his face was changed and his clothing became brilliant as lightning. Suddenly there were two men there talking with him; they were Moses and Elijah appearing in glory, and they were speaking of his passing which he was to accomplish in Jerusalem. And a voice came from the cloud saying, 'This is my beloved Son, listen to him.'

Luke 9:29-31,35

It was during his journey to Jerusalem that the Transfiguration of the Lord Jesus took place. The appearance of Moses and Elijah at his side bears witness to what he said elsewhere, that he had come not to destroy but to fulfil the Law and the Prophets [Mt 5:17]. By his approaching suffering, death and resurrection Christ would bring to perfection the divine plan as found in the Scriptures. Both Moses and Elijah encountered God on a mountain, and now they are found with the Son of God on the mount of Transfiguration. The promised One for whom they helped prepare the way had now come. It is to him that we must now listen. He is the supreme lawgiver and the greatest prophet of all. At the moment of Transfiguration Peter, James and John were quite overwhelmed, but the experience would remain with them, and Peter recalls it as an old man [2 Pt 1:16-18]. In the quietness of our hearts let us join the Lord Jesus on the holy mountain, hearing again in faith the Father's voice declaring that Jesus was his beloved Son.

PRAYER

Lord Jesus, you revealed yourself on the mountain in the presence of your disciples as the glorious Son of God. In you the Law of Moses and all the words of the prophets reached fulfilment. You are God's own Word spoken to us, and bringing from heaven the law of universal love. Lord, the memory of your transfiguration would sustain Peter, James and John in the trials which lay ahead of them, and they would later testify courageously before the world to the full truth of who you were. In the ordinariness of our daily lives, sustain and nurture our faith with the vision of your heavenly glory which you laid aside to become for us the Word made flesh.

'Lord Jesus, you bequeathed to the Church the sacrament of your body and blood as the supreme expression of your love...'

The Institution of the Eucharist

While they were eating, Jesus took bread, blessed and broke it, and gave it to his disciples saying, 'Take and eat, this is my body.' And taking the cup he gave thanks and gave it to them, saying, 'Drink all of you from this, for this is my blood, the blood of the covenant, which is to be poured out for many for the forgiveness of sins.' Matthew 26:26-28

It was the time of Passover when the Jews sacrificed the paschal lamb and recalled their deliverance by God from slavery in Egypt. Jesus and his disciples, faithful to the tradition of their ancestors, met to celebrate this meal. Conscious that the climax of his life was approaching, Christ gave a whole new meaning to this sacred celebration. Anticipating his death the following day, Good Friday, he gave his disciples another kind of food, his body and blood. Christ was showing that he was the true paschal lamb whose body would be broken on the cross and his blood poured out on Calvary, to take away the sins of the whole world. So great was his love for his disciples that he wanted them to share in his life-giving sacrifice by partaking of the sacred meal. This was the priceless gift of himself, the holy Eucharist, which Christ the Lord gave to his Church. In the words of St. Paul, 'Therefore, every time you eat this bread and drink this cup, you are proclaiming the death of the Lord until he comes' [1 Cor 11:26]. Whenever we are at Mass, let us resolve to approach this banquet and sacrifice of the Lord with profound love and deep reverence.

PRAYER

Lord Jesus, you bequeathed to the Church the sacrament of your body and blood as the supreme expression of your love. In this most intimate of meals you become one with us, while we become one with you and with each other. This is the holy food of travellers as they make their way to that great banquet your Father has prepared for us in his kingdom. Each time we gather around the altar we offer once more the sacrifice of the new and eternal covenant, sealed in your precious blood. Lord, our hearts are filled with wonder at this gift of the bread of life, the true manna which has come down from heaven. Let the unity of the Church be strengthened by the one bread of your body and the one cup of your blood. May the food of the holy Eucharist sustain us until we reach our heavenly homeland and come to that eternal feast which the Father has in store for all peoples.

The
Sorrowful
Mysteries

Pope John Paul II kneels in prayer at the Grotto

The Agony in the Garden

*And going out to a place called Gethsemane, he said to his disciples,
'Stay here while I go there to pray.' He took with him Peter, James and
John and began to be sorrowful and troubled. And he said to them, 'My
soul is sorrowful even to death. Stay here and keep watch with me.'*

Mark 14:32-34

Jesus had now come to the hour of which he had often spoken.
It was the hour of his struggle with Satan, the Prince of
darkness. The Gospels speak of his mental distress in the garden of
Gethsemane as he poured out his heart in prayer to his Father.
Humanly speaking he shrank from the suffering he knew that
struggle would involve, but obedience to his Father's will must
come first. In his Incarnation he left his divinity aside and humbled
himself to become one of us, to experience fear, pain and suffering
in order to redeem us. He willingly drank from the cup that was set
before him, while teaching us through his example to live the truth
of the petition of the prayer he taught: 'Thy will be done on earth,
as it is in heaven.'

PRAYER

Lord Jesus, in Gethsemane you knew what it was to be alone and
fearful. In your distress you entrusted yourself to your heavenly
Father and made his will your own. You were frightened of what
lay ahead, but a loving confidence in your Father enabled you to
embrace your Passion and the future. When we are afraid, and our
hearts are apprehensive at what lies before us, may we never lose
sight of your Father's infinite love for us. Give us a strong faith to
realise that as your Father was always at your side, so too he is never
far from any of his children.

'When the shadow of suffering falls across our path may we accept it patiently after your example.'

The Scourging at the Pillar

Pilate then had Jesus taken away and scourged. John 19:1

Jesus often spoke to his disciples about the sufferings that lay ahead of him. His words were coming to pass; he was now helpless and at the mercy of the Roman soldiers who scourged him. Long before, the prophet Isaiah described the servant of the Lord as bearing our sufferings and carrying our sorrows, [Is 53:4]. The Lord Jesus now fulfilled that prophecy, and it is through his bruises that we have been healed. He is the innocent Lamb of God who by his patient endurance takes away the sins of the world. Throughout his extreme ordeal Christ remained silent and did not retaliate, but placed his trust in the One who judges justly, his heavenly Father. Christ has suffered for us, leaving us an example to follow in his footsteps. May the imitation of the patient Christ be our rule of life.

PRAYER

Lord Jesus, through your humiliation and suffering you became the innocent Lamb of God who takes away the sins of the world. By your wounds we are healed, for you are the one who has truly borne our illnesses and carried our infirmities. Pour out your healing on a world so often afflicted with pain and distress. Help the sick to find hope in their sufferings by uniting them with yours for the salvation of the world. When the shadow of suffering falls across our path may we accept it patiently after your example.

'Lord Jesus... Through your innocent suffering you made atonement for the guilty.'

The Crowning with Thorns

The soldiers twisted some thorns into a crown and placed it on his head, and dressed him in a purple robe. They kept coming up to him and saying, 'Hail, king of the Jews!', slapping him in the face. John 19:2-3

As the drama of his passion unfolds, Christ now becomes the object of mockery and scorn. He, the king of kings, is humiliated and made a laughing-stock. Pilate seeks in vain to release Jesus and presents him to the people, but in the end gives way to those who wish to see him put to death. St Peter later remarks how a murderer was released while the Prince of life was put to death [Acts 3:15]. The rough ways of Roman justice were taking their course, yet mysteriously what God said through the prophet about his Messiah having to suffer was coming true: 'I have offered my back to those who struck me, my cheeks to those who tore at my beard; I have not turned my face away from insult and spitting.' [Is 50:6]. Even the darkest moments of Christ's suffering found their place in the Father's saving plan. We unite our moments of trouble and distress with those of Christ knowing that God can draw good from them.

PRAYER

Lord Jesus, you who went about doing good were ill-treated and scorned. You who will come again at the end of time to judge the living and the dead were yourself condemned to death. Through your innocent suffering you made atonement for the guilty. You, the Lord and master, came not to be served but to serve, and to offer your life as a ransom for us all. You said that there can be no greater love than for a man to lay down his life for his friends. You bore the burden of our sins, may we bear one another's burdens and so fulfil your law of love.

'I am the Immaculate Conception'

Jesus carries his Cross

They then took charge of Jesus, and bearing his own cross he went out to the place called the Skull, in Hebrew Golgotha. John 19:16-17

The evangelist, John, states that Jesus, now condemned to death, took up his own cross and went on his way to Calvary. Having the power to lay down his life and to take it up again, Jesus embraced the cross of his own free will, as an act of love freely undertaken for us all. The suffering Christ remained firmly in control of his own destiny, whatever the wicked might try to do to him. The way of the cross for him would prove to be his pathway to the glory of the resurrection, when the Father would reveal to the world the true identity of Jesus as his eternal Son. Jesus invites us to take up our cross and follow him. However heavy the cross might be he will shoulder its weight with us, for it is by sharing his sufferings that we will also share his glory.

PRAYER

Lord Jesus, the road to Calvary was, for you, a journey of humiliation and sorrow. Your received the sentence of a common criminal, a figure of reproach and contempt to those who saw you. Carrying your cross, it seemed as if your ministry of healing, peace and forgiveness had been to no avail. Yet weighed down by suffering and weakness you still acknowledged the tears and lament of the women of Jerusalem along the way to Calvary. Lord, teach us how to reach out to others in trouble, even in the midst of our own pain, for when we do so we are reaching out to you.

'Lord Jesus, we place all our hope in your cross, for it is the ark of our salvation...'

The Crucifixion

When they reached the place called The Skull, there they crucified him and the two criminals, one on his right, the other on his left. Jesus said, 'Father, forgive them, for they do not know what they are doing.'

Luke 23:33-34

With arms outstretched on the altar of the cross the Son of God offers himself to his Father as the supreme sacrifice for the salvation of the world. He has drunk the chalice of suffering to the full. He was born poor in a stable and now dies destitute and an outcast between two robbers. His act of self-humiliation is complete. Only his mother, the beloved disciple John, and a few others stayed faithful to the end. Everyone else had abandoned him. In keeping with his message of love and reconciliation, his final word was a prayer of forgiveness for those who had nailed him to the cross. This was his last and most powerful example to us of turning the other cheek. His life's work now complete, he surrendered himself into the hands of his Father. Following his example, we pray for the grace to be ministers of reconciliation in life, and in faith surrender ourselves into God's hands at the moment of our death.

PRAYER

Lord Jesus, through your life and sacred passion you glorified your Father on earth, and finished the work he gave you to do. On the cross you experienced death so that we might have life and have it in all its fullness. You were born of Mary as one of us, and dying on Calvary you embraced our common lot as sons and daughters of Adam. You entered the dark night of death, laying down your life only to take it up again on Easter morning. Lord Jesus, we place all our hope in your cross, for it is the ark of our salvation on which we pass across the waters of this life to the Promised Land of heaven. You were raised up on the cross; raise us up together with you and give us the fullness of life.

The
Glorious
Mysteries

Mass in the Underground Basilica – Lourdes

The Resurrection

The women found that the stone had been rolled away from the tomb, but on entering they could not find the body of the Lord Jesus. As they stood there puzzled about this, two men in brilliant clothes suddenly appeared at their side. Terrified, the women bowed their heads to the ground. But the two said to them, 'Why look among the dead for someone who is alive? He is not here; he has risen.' Luke 24:2-5

At dawn on the Sunday morning the faithful women came to the tomb to perform their final act of love for Jesus by anointing his body, only to discover that the stone had been rolled away and the tomb was empty. The Lord Jesus was no longer there. The angels declared that he had risen from the dead! The women were both frightened and overjoyed at what they were seeing and hearing. It was then that they began to realise that the terrible events of Good Friday did not signal the end for Jesus. They and the apostles would recall too that the Lord never referred to his passion and death without adding that he would rise from the dead after three days. They realised the truth of the Scriptures that God would not allow his Son to suffer the corruption of the grave [Ps 16:10]. Life had triumphed over death. Christ has risen from the dead, never to die again, assuring us that he remains with us always, to the end of time [Mt 28:20].

PRAYER

Lord Jesus, on Easter morning through the Father's infinite power you rose from the dead to the splendour of a new and incorruptible life. By your cross and resurrection you destroyed the ancient power of death and gave us the hope of an inheritance that will never perish or fade away. Renew and deepen our faith, Lord, in the truth of your resurrection, and make us fully aware that you are always with us here on earth, and also in the presence of your Father where you live to make intercession for us. Never let our troubles and difficulties overwhelm us for in you, the risen Lord, we are victorious in all things.

'Lord Jesus Christ, ...by your resurrection you delivered us from the power of darkness, and brought us into God's kingdom of light.'

The Ascension

Then he took them out as far as the outskirts of Bethany, and raising his hands he blessed them. Now as he blessed them, he withdrew from them and was carried up to heaven. Luke 24:50-51

The Lord Jesus had come from the Father into this world, and now he was leaving the world to return to his Father. During his life on earth, as a beloved Son, he had glorified his Father and through his death and resurrection completed the work he was given to do [Jn 17:4]. But his Ascension was not a final leave-taking from us. He would see his friends again because he was going ahead to prepare a place for them in order to bring them with him. Christ had now gone to take his proper place at the right hand of the Father, and as our supreme high-priest makes intercession for us at God's throne. We have his word that he will not abandon or forsake us. Christ our brother, the first-born from the dead, has now ascended to glory. Where he has gone, there we hope to follow.

PRAYER

Lord Jesus Christ, in your Ascension you returned to heaven, to the home of your Father. At his appointed time you were conceived in the womb of the Virgin Mary, becoming one with us in our human condition here on earth. Through your self-surrender to death on a cross and by your resurrection you delivered us from the power of darkness, and brought us into God's kingdom of light. Lord Jesus, keep our minds and hearts fixed on the things of heaven where you are now seated at the Father's right hand. We pray that when our earthly pilgrimage is over we may take our place with you in the glory which you have won for us by your cross.

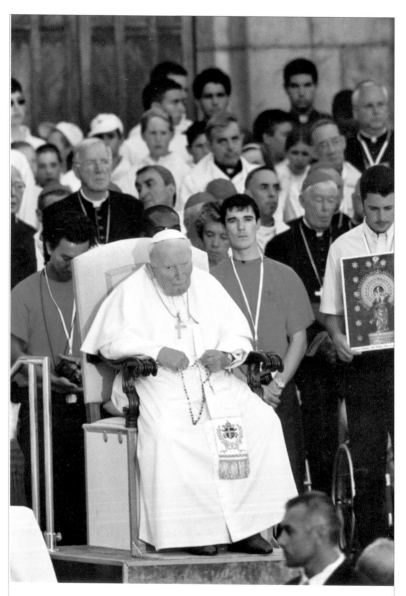

'May your love, poured into our hearts through the Holy Spirit,
help us to lead lives worthy of the grandeur of our
Christian vocation.' Pope John Paul II

The Descent of the Holy Spirit on the Disciples

Suddenly there came from heaven something like the sound of a mighty wind which filled the whole house where they were sitting. Then there appeared to them what seemed like tongues of fire, coming to rest separately on the heads of each one of them, and they were all filled with the Holy Spirit, and began to speak in tongues as the Spirit gave them the gift of speech. Acts 2:2-4

Obedient to the command of Jesus, the apostles and disciples remained in Jerusalem, with Mary in their midst, until they received the promised gift of the Father [Lk 24:49]. That promise was fulfilled when the Holy Spirit came down on them on Pentecost Day, and so the Church began. At creation the Holy Spirit drew order out of chaos, and later overshadowed the Virgin Mary, making possible the conception of the Son of God. The same Holy Spirit now calls into being God's new creation, the Church. Through the sin of pride at the tower of Babel [Gen 11], the human race was scattered and confused. At Pentecost the many nations present in Jerusalem listened to the marvels of God in their own language. We pray for a fresh outpouring of the Holy Spirit on the Church that the wonderful works of God may be made known again in our day.

PRAYER

Father in heaven, you anointed the apostles and disciples with the power of the Holy Spirit, whom Jesus promised would lead his Church in the ways of truth. Open our hearts to the gentle guidance of the Spirit, the Spirit who is the love of Father and Son. In times of doubt let the Spirit be our counsellor, in times of sadness our comforter, and in times of weakness our strength. Renew through the Holy Spirit the community of the baptised that your Church may truly be the light of the nations and a place of hope for all peoples.

'…You shared the joy and the pain of all mothers during your time on earth…'

The Assumption of Our Blessed Lady into Heaven

Henceforth all generations will call me blessed, for the Almighty has done great things for me. Holy is his name. Luke 1:49

The Church proclaims what has been her belief from earliest times that at the end of her earthly life the Virgin Mary was taken body and soul to heaven, there to share forever in the glory of her Son. The Scriptures relate how the Blessed Virgin Mary cooperated fully with God's plan for the salvation of the world. Beginning with her assent to the angel Gabriel at the Annunciation, Mary remained steadfastly faithful to her vocation as the mother of Christ. That fidelity was demonstrated above all when Mary stood at the foot of the cross, watching her Son suffer and die. The assurance of faith teaches us that Mary, conceived without original sin, did not suffer the decay of the grave, but by God's grace was made sharer in her son Christ's victory over sin and death. Mary is that exalted daughter of Zion, spoken of by the prophet Zephaniah [3:14-15], in whose midst the Lord came to dwell. She remains blessed among women because of the very special child whose mother she was. Now in glory, she remains our mother as well.

PRAYER

O Mary, mother of the Word incarnate, throughout your life you showed yourself to be the faithful servant of God. Always placing the divine will above your own, you associated yourself fully with the life and work of your divine Son, Jesus Christ. You shared the joy and the pain of all mothers during your time on earth, and from your place in heaven you continue to care for all who follow in the footsteps of your Son. Be a true mother to us on our pilgrimage through life. Protect us from all danger, so that like you we may persevere to the end in faith, hope and charity.

'As Queen and mother you are attentive to all who seek your help…'

The Coronation of Our Blessed Lady as Queen of Heaven

You are the glory of Jerusalem. You are the praise of Israel. You are the highest honour of our race. Judith 15:9

Throughout her life, Mary was truly the handmaid of the Lord. She was chosen by the Father in the fullness of time to be the mother of his divine Son, Jesus Christ. The great biblical figures and our ancestors in the faith: the patriarchs, prophets and kings each played their part in preparing the way for the birth of God's son. But it fell to Mary alone, through her motherhood, to enable the divine plan to reach fruition. Now honoured as the Queen of Saints in the glory of heaven, Our Blessed Lady is the advocate and protector of God's people as they make their pilgrim way to eternal life. On Calvary Jesus entrusted us to the care of Mary his mother. She continues to exercise her maternal care in our regard, and countless believers have found in her a true mother in their time of need. Our firm hope is that Mary, Queen of heaven, will pray for us now, and especially at the hour of our death.

PRAYER

O blessed mother, you are honoured in every part of the Catholic world. Those who follow the way of your Son in every age have always turned to you and poured out their hearts in prayer and supplication. As Queen and mother you are attentive to all who seek your help, reserving a special place for the humble and the downcast. You were one with your Son in his work of redemption, and stood by his side in the darkness of Calvary when he needed you most. Intercede for us now with your Son in heaven as we unite with many generations who have called you blessed.

HAIL HOLY QUEEN

Hail Holy Queen, Mother of Mercy,
hail our life, our sweetness and our hope!
To thee do we cry, poor banished children of Eve;
to thee do we send up our sighs,
mourning and weeping in this vale of tears.
Turn then, most gracious Advocate,
thine eyes of mercy towards us;
and after this our exile,
show unto us the blessed fruit of thy womb, Jesus.
O clement, O loving, O sweet Virgin Mary.

P. Pray for us, O holy Mother of God
R. That we may be made worthy of the promises of Christ.

SALVE REGINA

Salve Regina, Mater Misericordiæ:
vita, dulcedo et spes nostra salve.
Ad te clamamus, exsules filii, Hevae.
Ad te suspiramus gementes et flentes in hac lacrimarum valle.
Eia ergo, advocata nostra,
illos tuos misericordes oculos ad nos converte.
Et Jesum, benedictum fructum ventris tui,
nobis post hoc exsilium ostende.
O clemens, O pia, O dulcis Virgo Maria.

LITANY OF OUR LADY

Lord, have mercy	Lord, have mercy
Christ, have mercy	Christ, have mercy
Lord, have mercy	Lord, have mercy
Christ, hear us	Christ, graciously hear us
God the Father of Heaven	have mercy on us
God the Son, Redeemer of the World	have mercy on us
God the Holy Spirit	have mercy on us
Holy Trinity, one God	have mercy on us
Holy Mary	pray for us
Holy Mother of God	pray for us
Holy Virgin of virgins	pray for us
Mother of Christ	pray for us
Mother of Divine Grace	pray for us
Mother most pure	pray for us
Mother most chaste	pray for us
Mother inviolate	pray for us
Mother undefiled	pray for us
Mother most lovable	pray for us
Mother most admirable	pray for us
Mother of Good Counsel	pray for us
Mother of our creator	pray for us
Mother of our Saviour	pray for us
Virgin most prudent	pray for us
Virgin most venerable	pray for us
Virgin most renowned	pray for us
Virgin most powerful	pray for us
Virgin most merciful	pray for us
Virgin most faithful	pray for us
Mirror of justice	pray for us
Seat of Wisdom	pray for us
Cause of our joy	pray for us
Spiritual vessel	pray for us
Vessel of honour	pray for us
Singular vessel of devotion	pray for us
Mystical rose	pray for us
Tower of David	pray for us

Tower of ivory	pray for us
House of Gold	pray for us
Ark of the Covenant	pray for us
Gate of heaven	pray for us
Morning star	pray for us
Health of the sick	pray for us
Refuge of sinners	pray for us
Comfort of the afflicted	pray for us
Help of Christians	pray for us
Queen of angels	pray for us
Queen of patriarchs	pray for us
Queen of prophets	pray for us
Queen of apostles	pray for us
Queen of martyrs	pray for us
Queen of confessors	pray for us
Queen of virgins	pray for us
Queen of all saints	pray for us
Queen conceived without original sin	pray for us
Queen assumed into heaven	pray for us
Queen of the most holy Rosary	pray for us
Queen of the family	pray for us
Queen of peace	pray for us

Lamb of God, you take away the sins of the world	spare us, O Lord
Lamb of God, you take away the sins of the world	graciously hear us, O Lord
Lamb of God, you take away the sins of the world	have mercy on us

Pray for us, O holy Mother of God
That we may be worthy of the promises of Christ.

Let us pray:

Grant that we your servants, Lord, may enjoy unfailing health of mind and body, and through the prayers of the ever Blessed Virgin Mary in her glory, free us from our sorrows in this world and give us eternal happiness in the next. Through Christ our Lord. Amen.

At the end of the Rosary, in some cultures it is customary to recite the following prayer for the Holy Souls in Purgatory:

Eternal rest grant unto them, O Lord,
and let perpetual light shine upon them.
May they rest in peace.
Amen.

PRAYER TO
THE MOTHER OF GOOD COUNSEL

Mary, Our Mother, we thank you
that we can always call upon you
to help us in our need.

You were chosen from the whole human race
and entrusted by God, Creator of the Universe,
to nurture his Son, Jesus, and to guide his steps.
It is with confidence that we come to you now and,
pondering on how you held Jesus in your heart
and in your arms,
we ask you to hold us in the same way,
so that we can be close to you and to your Son.
Show us how to reveal Jesus to others
with gentleness and love,
and guide us with wisdom and good counsel
on our journeying through life.

Amen.

St Bernadette Soubirous

The Prayers of the Rosary

OUR FATHER

Our Father who art in heaven, hallowed be Thy name; Thy kingdom come; Thy will be done on earth as it is in heaven. Give us this day our daily bread; and forgive us our trespasses as we forgive those who trespass against us; and lead us not into temptation, but deliver us from evil. Amen.

HAIL MARY

Hail Mary, full of grace, the Lord is with thee. Blessed art thou amongst women and blessed is the fruit of thy womb, Jesus. Holy Mary, Mother of God, pray for us sinners, now and at the hour of our death. Amen.

GLORY BE TO THE FATHER

Glory be to the Father, and to the Son, and to the Holy Spirit. As it was in the beginning, is now, and ever shall be, world without end. Amen.

FATIMA PRAYER

(usually added after the Glory Be – at the end of each decade)

O my Jesus, forgive us our sins, save us from the fires of hell and bring all souls to heaven, especially those most in need of Thy mercy.

THE APOSTLES' CREED

I believe in God, the Father Almighty, Creator of heaven and earth; and in Jesus Christ, His only Son, our Lord; who was conceived by the Holy Spirit, born of the Virgin Mary, suffered under Pontius Pilate, was crucified, died, and was buried. He descended into hell; on the third day He rose again from the dead; He ascended into heaven and is seated at the right hand of God, the Father Almighty. Thence He shall come to judge the living and the dead. I believe in the Holy Spirit, the Holy Catholic Church, the Communion of Saints, the forgiveness of sins, the resurrection of the body, and life everlasting. Amen.

HAIL, HOLY QUEEN
(see p.57)

— · —

THE ANGELUS

P. The Angel of the Lord declared unto Mary
R. And she conceived of the Holy Spirit.

Hail Mary, full of grace...

P. Behold the handmaid of the Lord
R. Be it done unto me according to thy word.

Hail Mary, full of grace...

P. And the Word was made flesh
R. And dwelt among us.

Hail Mary, full of grace...

P. Pray for us, O holy mother of God
R. That we may be made worthy of the promises of Christ.

Let us pray:

Pour forth, we beseech thee O Lord, thy grace into our hearts, that we, to whom the incarnation of Christ Thy Son was made known by the message of an angel, may be brought by His Passion and Cross to the glory of his resurrection, through the same Christ our Lord. Amen.

PRAYER TO OUR LADY OF LOURDES

Ever Immaculate Virgin, Mother of mercy,
health of the sick, refuge of sinners, comfort of the afflicted,
you know our needs, our troubles, our sufferings.
Cast on me a look of pity.
By appearing in the Grotto of Lourdes,
you were pleased to make it a privileged sanctuary,
from which you dispense your favours,
and already many sufferers have obtained the cure of
their infirmities, both spiritual and physical.
We come, therefore, with the most unbounded confidence to
implore your maternal intercession.
Obtain most loving Mother, our requests, through Jesus Christ
your Son, our Lord. Amen.

THE MEMORARE

Remember, O most loving Virgin Mary,
that it is a thing unheard of,
that anyone who ever had recourse to your protection,
implored your help, or sought your intercession,
was left forsaken.
Filled therefore with confidence in your goodness
I fly to you, O Mother, Virgin of virgins,
to you I come, before you I stand, a sorrowful sinner.
Despise not my poor words, O Mother of the Word of God,
but graciously hear and grant my prayer.
Amen.

Pope John Paul II

THE MAGNIFICAT

My soul glorifies the Lord,
my spirit rejoices in God, my Saviour.
He looks on his servant in her lowliness;
henceforth all ages will call me blessed.

The Almighty works marvels for me.
Holy is his name.
His mercy is from age to age,
on those who fear him.

He puts forth his arm in strength
and scatters the proud-hearted.
He casts the mighty from their thrones
and raises the lowly.

He fills the starving with good things,
sends the rich away empty.

He protects Israel, his servant,
remembering his mercy,
the mercy promised to our fathers,
to Abraham and his sons for ever.

SUB TUUM PRAESIDIUM

Sub tuum praesidium confugimus, sancta Dei Genitrix:
Nostras deprecationes ne despicias in necessitatibus,
Sed a periculis cunctis libera nos semper,
Virgo gloriosa et benedicta.

We fly to thy protection, O Holy Mother of God.
Despise not our petitions in our necessities,
but deliver us always from all dangers
O glorious and blessed Virgin.

ALMA REDEMPTORIS MATER

Alma Redemptoris Mater,
Quae pervia cœli porta manes, et stella maris,
Succurre cadenti, surgere qui curat, populo;
Tu quae genuisti, natura mirante,
Tuum sanctum Genitorem,
Virgo prius ac posterius,
Gabrielis ab ore sumens illud Ave,
Peccatorum miserere.

Mother of Christ, hear thou thy people's cry.
Star of the sea and portal of the sky.
Sinking we strive and call to thee for aid.
Mother of him who thee from nothing made,
O by that joy which Gabriel brought to thee,
Thou, Virgin first and last, let us thy mercy see.

AVE REGINA CAELORUM

Ave, Regina Cælorum,
Ave, Domina Angelorum:
Salve radix, salve porta,
Ex qua mundo lux est orta.
Gaude, Virgo gloriosa,
Super omnes speciosa;
Vale, o valde decora,
Et pro nobis Christum exora.

Hail, O Queen of Heaven enthroned,
Hail, as queen of angels owned.
Root of Jesse, gate of morn,
whence the world's true light was born.
Glorious Virgin, joy to thee,
the loveliest in heaven to see.
Fairest thou where all are fair,
plead with Christ our sins to spare.

V. Grant that I may give you worthy praise, O Holy Virgin.
R. Give me strength against all your enemies.

Let us pray:

Give us help in our weakness, O merciful God, so that as we keep holy the memory of the Mother of God, by the help of her intercession we may be saved from our sins; through Jesus Christ our Lord. Amen.

REGINA COELI

Regina cœli, laetare, Alleluia,
Quia quem meruisti portare, Alleluia
Resurrexit sicut dixit, Alleluia
Ora pro nobis Deum, Alleluia

Queen of heaven, rejoice, Alleluia
For he whom thou didst merit to bear, Alleluia
Has risen as he said, Alleluia,
Pray for us to God, Alleluia

V. Rejoice and be glad O Virgin Mary, Alleluia
R. For the Lord has risen indeed, Alleluia

Let us pray:
O God, who by the resurrection of your Son our Lord Jesus Christ
has given joy to the whole world: grant that through the help of his
mother we may obtain the joys of everlasting life, through the
same Jesus Christ our Lord. Amen.

CONSECRATION TO MARY MOST HOLY,
QUEEN OF THE APOSTLES

Receive me, Mary, Teacher and Queen,
among those whom thou dost love and guide
in the school of thy Son, the Divine Master.
As thy Son placed Himself in thy care,
I give myself entirely into thy hands.
Obtain for me the grace to know, imitate and love ever more
my Divine Master,
the Way, the Truth and the Life.
Speak for me to thy Son, for I am an unworthy sinner.
Enlighten my mind, fortify my will, sanctify my heart,
so that I may be able to say at its conclusion,
I live, no not I, but Christ liveth in me.

Immaculate Mary!
Our hearts are on fire,
that title so wondrous
fills all our desire

Ave, ave, ave Maria!
Ave, ave, ave Maria!

We pray for God's glory,
may His kingdom come!
We pray for his Vicar,
our Father, and Rome.

Ave, ave, ave Maria!
Ave, ave, ave Maria!

We pray for our Mother,
the Church upon earth,
and bless, sweetest Lady,
the land of our birth.

Ave, ave, ave Maria!
Ave, ave, ave Maria!

For poor, sick, afflicted
thy mercy we crave;
and comfort the dying
thou light of the grave.

Ave, ave, ave Maria!
Ave, ave, ave Maria!

There is no need, Mary,
nor ever has been,
which thou canst not succour,
Immaculate Queen.

Ave, ave, ave Maria!
Ave, ave, ave Maria!

In grief and temptation,
in joy or in pain,
we'll ask thee, our Mother,
nor seek thee in vain.

Ave, ave, ave Maria!
Ave, ave, ave Maria!

O bless us, Dear Mother
with blessings from heaven.
And to our petitions
let answer be given.

Ave, ave, ave Maria!
Ave, ave, ave Maria!

In death's solemn moment,
our Mother, be nigh;
as children of Mary –
O teach us to die.

Ave, ave, ave Maria!
Ave, ave, ave Maria!

And crown thy sweet mercy
with this special grace,
to behold soon in heaven
God's ravishing face.

Ave, ave, ave Maria!
Ave, ave, ave Maria!

To God be all glory
and worship for aye,
and to God's Virgin Mother
an endless Ave.

Ave, ave, ave Maria!
Ave, ave, ave Maria!